English Skills
Teacher's Guide

Carol Matchett

Schofield & Sims

Published by Schofield & Sims Ltd,
Dogley Mill, Fenay Bridge, Huddersfield HD8 0NQ, UK
Telephone 01484 607080

www.schofieldandsims.co.uk

British Library Cataloguing in Publication Data
A catalogue record for this book is available from the British Library.

Commissioning and editorial project management by
Carolyn Richardson Publishing Services (www.publiserve.co.uk)

Design by **Ledgard Jepson Ltd**
Printed in the UK by **Wyndeham Gait Ltd**, Grimsby, Lincolnshire

ISBN 978 07217 1187 4

Contents

1. Introduction

Description

English Skills

Schofield & Sims English Skills provides regular and carefully graded practice in key literacy skills. Comprising six workbooks with accompanying books of answers, plus this one **Teacher's Guide** covering the whole series, it is designed primarily for Key Stage 2 pupils.

This **Teacher's Guide** introduces the series, describes three different methods for selecting the right workbook for each pupil or class, and explains how the workbooks are best used on a day-to-day basis. Two sets of resources are also provided. The **Assessment resources** support you, the teacher, in your selection of the most appropriate workbook. The **General resources** provide a **Group record sheet**. They also include a variety of other useful resources that will help you to develop pupils' spelling, vocabulary and punctuation skills and to set literacy targets for them – which they can then monitor themselves.

Essential English Skills

By popular request, Schofield & Sims provides the **English Skills** workbooks in an alternative format – for use at Key Stage 3 and beyond with students who may be struggling with the work normally given to their age-group. The content of this second set of workbooks is exactly the same, but the covers are designed for older students and bear the slightly revised title, **Essential English Skills**. The **English Skills** books of answers are fully compatible with the **Essential English Skills** workbooks. Similarly the content of this **Teacher's Guide** is as applicable to **Essential English Skills** as it is to the main **English Skills** series.

A full list of all **English Skills** and **Essential English Skills** books is provided at the back of this guide.

The 'I can do' teaching method

Below the list of **English Skills** books at the back of the **Teacher's Guide** you will find a reference to the **I can do** teaching method. This is one way of using a workbook series such as **English Skills** to provide pupils with intensive daily practice. If you are interested in exploring the method, which is essentially the same whatever the subject being taught, you can watch a specially-made film about **I can do maths** on the Schofield & Sims website **www.schofieldandsims.co.uk**: select **numeracy** at Key Stage 2 and **I can do maths**, then scroll down to find the video link.

Purpose

English Skills is for use alongside your existing literacy lessons, embedding key aspects of grammar, sentence structure, punctuation and spelling and constantly revisiting them until they become automatic. At the same time it reinforces and develops pupils' knowledge of word structure and vocabulary, encouraging them to develop an active interest in words, their meanings and how they work.

Pupils using **English Skills** are continually developing and refining the skills that they need in order to communicate ideas effectively. They learn how sentences are formed and manipulated and how words are selected and combined.

The series also introduces pupils to the technical terms needed to talk about language, developing their vocabulary so that they can discuss what makes writing effective and how they can improve their own work. A short **Glossary** appears on the inside front cover of every workbook. A full photocopiable glossary covering the whole series is supplied at the back of this **Teacher's Guide**.

The importance of literacy skills

The ability to create and punctuate sentences and to use a range of strategies to spell words is vital to successful written composition. If these basic skills are not automatic and secure, then composition is difficult. When pupils have to focus primarily on grammar, spelling and punctuation, their attention is drawn away from the content and meaning of their writing. Composition will be slow and there will be no fluency in the writing or in the ideas expressed. As a result, pupils will lack confidence and writing will not be an enjoyable task.

Once these aspects of writing are automatic, however, writing becomes more fluent. The writer is free to concentrate on what he or she wants to say and has all the tools needed to communicate effectively. Pupils feel confident in their own abilities as writers; as a result, they are eager to 'have a go' and thoroughly enjoy writing.

Grammar, punctuation and spelling

Time and regular practice are needed to consolidate the key skills required for structuring sentences effectively and using the correct punctuation and spelling. **English Skills** provides ample opportunities for intensive practice, building pupils' fluency and confidence.

Vocabulary

Another vital ingredient of successful writing is a plentiful store of words to draw upon. **English Skills** helps pupils to develop a wide vocabulary, encouraging them to think carefully about word choice and to tailor their words to the needs of the reader. This enables the pupils to express their ideas clearly and effectively. Those pupils who are 'switched on' to words ask about their meaning, enjoy collecting words and use interesting new words in their own writing, even if they are not sure of the spelling. They experiment with different ways of expressing themselves and revise each sentence before, during and after writing.

Structure

The six workbooks are carefully graded from **English Skills 1** to **English Skills 6** to ensure progression in literacy skills.

Each workbook comprises three sections with 12 tests in each one. The tests become more difficult, but the increase in difficulty is gradual. The workbooks are fully compatible with the Key Stage 2 literacy curriculum and the final tests in each book are aligned with the end-of-year objectives for Years 2 to 7, as described on page 9 (see **Method 1**).

Please note: Pupils working towards the objectives for an earlier year should use the appropriate workbook. There is no need for all members of the class to be working on the same book at the same time.

Part A: **Warm-up** questions: word puzzles and other activities that focus on areas covered earlier.

Part B: **Word work** questions covering **spelling, word structure** and **vocabulary**.

Part C: **Sentence work** questions covering **sentence formation, punctuation** and **grammar**.

Some questions have more than one correct answer, and these are indicated using a simple key.

Section 1   Test 8

A   WARM-UP

Continue the sentence using a powerful verb.

1 The thunder _____

2 The flames _____

3 Shadows _____

Add the suffix **y** and write the new word.

4 guilt   _____

5 sparkle   _____

6 nut   _____

7 What sort of words have you made? Underline the correct answer.

   nouns   verbs   adjectives

Is the statement a fact or an opinion?

8 Matthews was the best player on the pitch.   _____

9 Paris is the capital city of France.   _____

10 Everyone loves the snow.   _____

B   WORD WORK

Underline the word in **bold** that fits the sentence.

1 It was a **super supper** day out.

2 It tasted **biter bitter**.

3 We had **diner dinner** at six.

4 How did you know how each word sounds?

   _____

   _____

5 Add the correct suffix to make the words into adjectives.

   al ic y ing

   rhythm____   sensation____

   music____   sport____

   athlete____   amaze____

Write the words as pairs of near synonyms.

6 _____ and _____

7 _____ and _____

8 _____ and _____

Write three synonyms.

9   run   _____ _____ _____

10 walk _____ _____ _____

C   SENTENCE WORK

Choose an adverb to add to the sentence.

gracefully neatly excitedly tearfully

1 The crowd shouted _____.

2 He folded the clothes _____.

3 The Princess begged _____.

4 The dancer curtseyed _____.

5 Put the phrases in order, using 1 for the shortest amount of time and 4 for the longest.

   an hour passed   ____   a few days later   ____

   after a few seconds   ____   minutes ticked by   ____

6 Write two phrases showing that even more time has passed.

   _____   _____

Complete these predictions about your future.

7   Tomorrow I _____

8   Later this week I _____

9   Later today I _____

10 Next week I _____

X There is only one correct answer.   X There is more than one correct answer.

11

This page is from **English Skills 3**.

Parts A, B and C

Every test is divided into three parts, with 10 questions in each:

- Part A: **Warm-up** – word puzzles, 'warm-up' exercises and revision of earlier learning

- Part B: **Word work** – spelling, word structure, exploring words and their meanings

- Part C: **Sentence work** – putting words together to make sentences: for example, choosing suitable words, forming and punctuating sentences or checking for grammatical accuracy.

Personalised learning

English Skills makes it easy for you to provide differentiated work for different abilities within a class or group. Pupils working significantly above or below age-related expectations may work on the book best suited to their needs. This means that all pupils will be working at their own level and pace. The more able will extend their knowledge and skills, while the less able will have time to reinforce earlier learning rather than struggling to keep up with general class sessions.

The **English Skills** workbooks provide a permanent record of work, and pupils are encouraged both to monitor their own progress and to take a pride in their work.

2. Getting started

This section describes three different methods for choosing the most appropriate **English Skills** workbook to use with each pupil.

You can use one or a combination of these methods to help you decide on the most suitable workbook. As stated earlier, there is no need for all members of the class to be working on the same book at the same time, particularly if you have a class with mixed ability levels.

All three methods for choosing the correct workbook require you to exercise your professional judgement. Whatever method you choose, you should always ensure that the book choice indicated concurs with your knowledge and understanding of the pupil's capabilities.

Method 1: Using end-of-year expectations

All the **English Skills** workbooks are fully compatible with the Key Stage 2 National Curriculum for English. They are aligned with end-of-year expectations as follows:

- **English Skills 1:** Year 2
- **English Skills 3:** Year 4
- **English Skills 5:** Year 6
- **English Skills 2:** Year 3
- **English Skills 4:** Year 5
- **English Skills 6:** Years 6/7

In the majority of cases, you will simply choose the book designed for the relevant year group. However, some pupils will be working significantly above or below age-related expectations. Where this is the case, the books should be assigned according to each pupil's current ability and needs rather than his or her age or year group. An outline of the content of each workbook is provided at the start of the **Assessment resources** section, so that you can see exactly what is covered in each one.

Use any assessment information that you have available – for example, from assessment for learning (AFL) profiles and assessing pupils' progress (APP) records – to make informed judgements about whether pupils are performing above, at or below age expectations. Then choose the workbook accordingly.

Method 2: Using the 'best fit' Workbook descriptors

Best fit Workbook descriptors are provided on pages 28 to 33. These set out:

- what a pupil starting each book **is already able to do** (in the form of 'can' statements relating to word and sentence level work)

- what the pupil **needs to work on next** in order to improve his or her skills (in the form of bullet-point targets relating to sentence structure, punctuation, grammar, spelling and word structure).

Use existing AFL information or a sample of every pupil's independent writing to get a picture of both their current strengths (what they can already do) and their weaknesses (what they need to learn next). The photocopiable **Writing sample assessment sheet** will help you to assess an existing sample.

If you do not have a writing sample – if the pupil has just arrived at your school, for example – use the writing tasks provided in this book as photocopy masters. **Writing task: Advert for a new car** and **Writing task: Jam sandwich!** are adapted from **English Skills 3** and **English Skills 4** respectively. A photocopiable **Writing task assessment sheet** has been specially designed for each of these tasks and will help you to record the pupil's current abilities and weaknesses in key areas.

Once you have a clear picture of the pupil's abilities, read through the best fit Workbook descriptors for each book to find the one that is closest to the pupil's current abilities and needs. This will tell you which workbook is best suited to the pupil.

Method 3: Using the Entry tests

The **Assessment resources** section of this guide also contains photocopiable Entry tests. These provide a third possible method of finding the right workbook for each pupil. There are five discrete tests, with 20 questions in each. **Entry tests 1** to **5** become increasingly challenging, **Entry test 1** being the most straightforward and **Entry test 5** the most difficult.

Entry test content

Each test comprises 10 word and 10 sentence questions, which relate to the statements in the best fit Workbook descriptors. The word questions test the pupil's ability in spelling and knowledge of word structure. The sentence questions test his or her ability in constructing sentences, using punctuation and grammar and choosing appropriate vocabulary.

Every test focuses on the bullet list of items that the pupil now needs to practise, as listed in the parallel Workbook descriptors. So, for example:

- **Entry test 1** focuses on the bullet lists of items in the Workbook descriptors for **English Skills 1**

- **Entry test 2** focuses on the bullet lists of items in the Workbook descriptors for **English Skills 2**

and so on.

Which test?

Normally pupils should not need to tackle all five tests. If you are confident that a pupil is beyond the basic level required in **Entry test 1**, he or she can begin with a later test.

Please note: Wherever possible, avoid situations where a pupil may need to sit more than three tests.

Pupils gain confidence from answering some simpler questions. For this reason, it is usually best to start the pupil on a test that is a little easier than the one that you expect him or her to be capable of completing successfully. However, if you think that a pupil is likely to need **English Skills 4**, **5** or **6**, do not start him or her at **Entry test 1** or he or she may lose concentration and become increasingly careless.

If you do administer **Entry test 1**, ensure that the pupil stops as soon as he or she begins to find the questions difficult or is making a large number of mistakes.

Before the test session, photocopy the Entry tests that you think you may need. For example, if your initial assessment is that a pupil will need **Entry test 2** or **3** you might photocopy **Entry tests 1**, **2** and **3**.

If you are administering the test to older students, with whom you plan to use the **Essential English Skills** workbooks, you may wish to use the **Essential English Skills** Entry tests, downloadable from the Schofield & Sims website (www.schofieldandsims.co.uk).

Their content is the same as the **English Skills** Entry tests, but they show the alternative series title.

Administering the Entry tests

The following simple steps will ensure that the Entry tests are fair and that pupils perform to the best of their ability in them.

- Explain to the pupils the purpose of the Entry tests: to find the workbook that is most appropriate to their individual skills and will be neither too easy nor too difficult for them.

- Instruct each pupil to write his or her name, class (or set) and date in the spaces provided at the top of each sheet.

- Tell the class members that they are to fill in the answer to each question in the space provided on the page. They must not write anything in the score boxes.

- Encourage the pupils to do their best but not to worry if there is something they don't understand or can't do yet. The purpose of the test is to make sure that they are given work at an appropriate level in future.

- Tell the pupils that they must work on the test independently and unaided.

- Ensure that the pupils know that these are not timed tests.

- Remind the pupils that it is important to concentrate, as small errors in punctuation and spelling will result in lost marks.

- (For pupils working on **Entry test 1** only:) Inform the pupils that you will read aloud to them the first one or two questions to help familiarise them with the process of following instructions. You may also introduce some of the key words and instructional language used: for example, **complete**, **underline**, **correct**.

- (For pupils working on **Entry tests 2** to **5** only:) Clarify for the pupils that they will receive no help with reading the questions or following the instructions, as these activities form part of the test. The reading level required and language used gradually become more challenging as the test continues.

Please note: The Entry tests use some basic literacy terms, such as **adjective**, **noun** and **clause**. The introduction of this language is carefully graded and reflects the use of these terms in the workbooks. Do not explain these terms to pupils, as understanding of the terms is part of the test.

Marking

An Entry test marking key is provided for each separate Entry test, to facilitate marking. All the Entry test marking keys appear in the **Assessment resources** section of this book. You may photocopy the marking keys if you wish – in black-and-white if necessary. If you do not have access to a colour printer, you may find it easier to use the two-colour versions contained in this book.

In the Entry test marking keys, a distinction is made, as in the **English Skills** books of answers, between those questions that have only one correct answer and those where more than one would be acceptable. Where a single definitive answer is not appropriate, a sample answer is given. Please note that this answer is for your guidance only – in some cases there will be many possible alternatives. The Entry tests themselves do **not** distinguish between questions with one or more than one answer as this would cause unnecessary distraction in the test situation.

As in the **English Skills** books of answers, **Focus** panels are provided on each Entry test marking key. These indicate the area or areas of learning being tested and help you to decide whether a pupil's answer is satisfactory.

Scoring

One full mark is available for each of the 20 questions in a test. You write the mark awarded in the score box to the right of each question.

There are two situations in which you might need to allocate half a mark.

- Some questions test more than one area: for example, a question on writing a sentence might also check pupils' knowledge of punctuation. In such cases, the **Focus** statement will make it clear that there are two different points for consideration. Both points must be covered by the answer if a full mark is to be allocated. This reflects real-life writing situations where knowledge and skills in different areas have to be drawn together. If only one aspect of the question has been answered correctly, award half a mark. For example, in a proofreading question, where the pupil has to spot various errors, one error might relate to the use of **ed** endings and another to the spelling of a high-frequency word. Both errors must be found if the pupil is to obtain the full mark.

- Other questions, typically in the **Word work** section, require pupils to write or spell two or more words. Usually, all the words in these questions are testing the same **Focus** point: for example, applying a spelling rule or knowledge of a prefix. Because more than one example is needed if the pupil is to demonstrate fully his or her understanding, all the words must be correct to get the full mark.

When you have finished marking the questions, add up the marks given and write the total score in the box in the bottom right-hand corner of the sheet.

A percentage score for each test may be worked out easily if required: simply multiply the total score by five and write it in the far left-hand box.

Interpretation of scores

If a pupil scores particularly well (achieving 15 or more marks) on the first test that you give him or her, he or she should proceed to the next test. The basic principle of the Entry tests is that pupils continue in this way until you find their upper ceiling and they start getting questions wrong: this tells you the book that they need.

If a pupil's score is in the mid-range (between 4 and 14), he or she should start on the workbook relating to that part of the test. There are key skills and areas of knowledge covered in that workbook that the pupil still needs to work on. For example, a pupil scoring 13 on **Entry test 3** should be allocated **English Skills 3**.

If a pupil scores very poorly (achieving 3 marks or less) on a test, he or she should be given the previous workbook for reinforcement. This way you can make sure that the pupil is confident with the earlier skills and knowledge before moving on. However, if the same pupil has already scored 15 to 20 on the earlier test then he or she should be moved quickly to the next book. For example, a pupil scoring 2 on **Entry test 3** should be given **English Skills 2** for reinforcement. If he or she has already obtained a high score (of 15, for example) on **Entry test 2**, he or she should be moved on quickly to **English Skills 3**.

Please refer to the **Score interpretation table** (below) for specific guidance. For easy reference, the relevant parts of this table are reproduced in the top right-hand corner of every Entry test marking key under the heading **Next steps**.

Once you have decided on the next step for a particular pupil, complete one of the middle two boxes at the foot of the Entry test sheet (for example, 'give pupil **English Skills 2**' or 'administer **Entry test 4**').

Score interpretation table

Test	Total score	Next steps
Entry test 1	0–3	pupil may not yet be ready to start **English Skills**
	4–14	give pupil **English Skills 1**
	15–20	administer **Entry test 2**
Entry test 2	0–3	give pupil **English Skills 1** for reinforcement; if pupil scored 15–20 on **Entry test 1**, move quickly to **English Skills 2**
	4–14	give pupil **English Skills 2**
	15–20	administer **Entry test 3**
Entry test 3	0–3	give pupil **English Skills 2** for reinforcement; if pupil scored 15–20 on **Entry test 2**, move quickly to **English Skills 3**
	4–14	give pupil **English Skills 3**
	15–20	administer **Entry test 4**
Entry test 4	0–3	give pupil **English Skills 3** for reinforcement; if pupil scored 15–20 on **Entry test 3**, move quickly to **English Skills 4**
	4–14	give pupil **English Skills 4**
	15–20	administer **Entry test 5**
Entry test 5	0–3	give pupil **English Skills 4** for reinforcement; if pupil scored 15–20 on **Entry test 4**, move quickly to **English Skills 5**
	4–14	give pupil **English Skills 5**
	15–20	give pupil **English Skills 5** for reinforcement; move quickly to **English Skills 6**

A word of caution

The Entry tests give only a brief snapshot of a pupil's knowledge and understanding in a range of areas. It is always a good idea to follow up the tests with a writing task (see **Method 2**, page 9). This will help you to assess more thoroughly the pupil's knowledge and understanding of the areas listed in the **Focus** panels and his or her ability to apply this knowledge when writing.

3. Using the workbooks

Introducing English Skills

Once you have decided to use **English Skills** in your class, you may find the following guidelines useful.

Before the first session

• You may wish to use the photocopiable **Group record sheet** provided in this guide (see start of **General resources** section) to keep a note of pupils' achievements. Before you start, record on the sheet the number of the highest Entry test that each pupil has taken – and the pupil's test score. Also note the number of the book that the pupil is to begin working through. If you are using **Essential English Skills**, an alternative **Group record sheet** is available online with the slightly revised title.

• Check that you have the **English Skills** workbooks that you need for each pupil in your class. You will also find it useful to have one copy each of the relevant books of answers. A full list of titles and ISBNs is available at the back of this guide.

Beginning the first session

• Invite each pupil to write his or her name and class (or set) in the space provided on the front cover.

• Tell the class members that they are to fill in the answer to each question in the space provided on the page.

• Point out that, because the pages are packed with all kinds of different questions, there is not a great deal of space for answers and so the pupils will need to write neatly. Generally the response lines should provide enough space, but those pupils who have larger handwriting may allow their answers to flow into other spaces on the sheet if absolutely necessary.

• You may feel that it is appropriate to explain to the class at this stage that if all or part of a question has several possible answers, the question number is displayed like this 5 . If a question has a specific answer, the question number is displayed like this 5 . It is displayed in this way even if the answer is made up of several parts that may be given in any order.

• You should also make it clear that pupils do not need to concern themselves about this labelling of different question types as they work through the test questions. Its primary purpose will be as an aid to marking – whether this is carried out by the pupils themselves, by a classroom assistant or by you, the teacher.

• Make sure the pupils know that these are not timed tests.

Please note: Before the pupils start work, you should demonstrate to the class the mechanics of how some of the different question types are to be answered. Concentrate on those question types that, from your knowledge of the pupils' abilities, you believe may be most challenging for them.

English Skills sessions

The pupils work through the test items without adult help – either individually or in pairs. For **English Skills 2** to **English Skills 6**, encourage them to refer to dictionaries, thesauruses and other reference materials rather than asking for your help. The tests may be used flexibly. For example, a test may be tackled in one session or over several days.

It is helpful if an environment that is conducive to literacy is established in the classroom. This will give pupils easy access to resources such as dictionaries at an appropriate level and posters displaying helpful examples and reminders. Many such items are available from Schofield & Sims: visit **www.schofieldandsims.co.uk** for further details. In addition, a range of photocopiable resources are supplied in this guide in the section **General resources**.

For example, you can use the three photocopiable **Vocabulary collection** sheets supplied to encourage pupils to become 'word collectors'. Suggest that they note on the sheets any words that they meet in the workbooks which might be useful in their own writing. Please see the Contents page for a full list of **General resources**.

Marking

A book of answers is provided to accompany every workbook in the series.

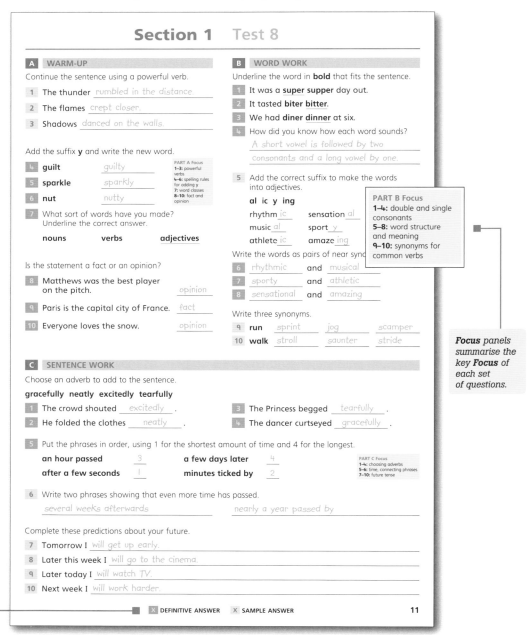

Focus panels summarise the key Focus of each set of questions.

Some questions have more than one correct answer, and these are indicated using a simple key.

This page is from **English Skills 3**.

Definitive and sample answers

As in the workbooks, a distinction is made in the books of answers between those questions that have only one correct answer and those where more than one would be acceptable. Where a single definitive answer is not appropriate, a sample answer is given: please note that this is for your guidance only – in some cases there will be many possible alternatives.

Please note: In a few instances there will be grey areas where there are possible alternatives even to answers that are labelled definitive. For example, there may be a completely different way of interpreting a question, or the use of a word may have changed over time. Although definitive-answer questions have been kept as tight and specific as possible at the time of writing, you should always use your discretion in marking – and refer to the **Focus** panels as described below.

Focus panels

One **Focus** panel is provided for every Part within each test, with separate **Focus** points given for each batch of questions. The **Focus** panel states the areas of learning being tested and is designed to help you decide whether the pupil's answer is satisfactory.

Some questions test more than one area: for example, a question on writing in the past tense might also check pupils' knowledge of the spelling rules for adding **ed**. In such cases, both parts of the answer must be correct, reflecting real-life situations that require varied knowledge and skills.

Group marking sessions

Group or class marking sessions led by the teacher or classroom assistant are the most effective way of marking the tests: pupils learn by comparing and discussing answers.

Another benefit of group or class marking sessions is that they highlight deficits in pupils' knowledge, which will inform your future teaching. Where pupils have given a wrong answer, or none at all, briefly reinforce the key teaching point using another item from the same book as a model. In a plenary discussion at the end of the session encourage pupils to evaluate their own successes; each pupil can then work with a 'talk partner' to record areas needing improvement and discuss appropriate learning objectives.

Suggested questions to ask in a marking session

- How many different 'correct' answers did we come up with?
- Were some sentence or word choices more interesting or effective than others? Why?
- How do you know this answer is correct?
- How can we make the answer correct?
- Is there an answer that would be even better?
- What are the success criteria for this type of question?
- What are the key points to remember next time?
- When might we put these key points into practice in our reading or writing?

Marking the end-of-section assessments

At the end of each workbook section are two writing assessments: the independent writing task and the proofreading task. These check that pupils are applying in their writing the knowledge, skills and understanding developed in the tests. The assessments also provide evidence of a pupil's strengths and weaknesses, which will help you to set appropriate targets. You might consider sharing with the pupils a simplified version of the mark scheme – and then involve them in setting their own targets, as discussed above.

- *The independent writing task*
  The independent writing task gives you a snapshot of a pupil's writing development. Prompts help pupils to plan and gather ideas so that when they begin writing they can focus on expressing their ideas clearly and effectively. On pages 16, 30 and 44 of each book of answers you will find photocopiable **Writing task assessment sheets** – one for each section – with specific assessment points arranged under the headings 'Sentence structure and punctuation', 'Composition and effect' and 'Spelling'. Complete one of these sheets as you mark each pupil's work.

  Sample writing tasks and **Writing task assessment sheets** are provided in this book as photocopy masters: see the **Assessment resources** section.

- *The proofreading task*
  The proofreading task focuses on punctuation, grammar and spelling. Examples of **Completed proofreading tasks** for each section, also photocopiable, are supplied on pages 17, 31 and 45 of each book of answers. However, please note that pupils may choose to correct some of the errors using methods different to those shown in the example but equally valid. For example, two unpunctuated strings of words might be joined using a connective or separated to make two sentences. Additional evidence gained from the relevant proofreading task will help you to further assess pupils' achievements in 'Sentence punctuation' and 'Spelling' as already assessed in the writing task. If you wish, you can use the photocopiable sheet to make notes on a pupil's work.

> **Please note**: Pupils whose scores against the assessment statements are low do not need to repeat a section. All the books revisit difficult areas and offer ample opportunities for further practice. Instead of holding a pupil back, highlight the assessment statements that reveal his or her weaknesses and use these to set learning targets. Ensure that pupils know their targets as they begin the next section.

Record-keeping, progression and targets

Record-keeping

As mentioned earlier, you can use the photocopiable **English Skills Group record sheet**, provided in this guide, to keep a note of pupils' achievements; an alternative version is available online for **Essential English Skills** users. The **Group record sheet** provides space for you to record pupils' marks on every test in each workbook.

Progress chart

English Skills helps you to set clear targets for each pupil. On page 46 of each pupil workbook you will find a **Progress chart** (see example opposite), with one column each for Sections 1, 2 and 3, and a list of 'I can' statements relating to the kinds of activities

English Skills 3 Progress chart

Name		Class/Set	
Teacher's name		Date	

Instructions

Read the **'I can' targets** for the section you have just finished.

- Colour the circle **green** if you find it **easy** to do what is described.
- Colour the circle **orange** if you are **getting there**, but still need to work on it.
- Colour the circle **red** if you still find this a **difficult** thing to do.

If there are things that you still find difficult you can work on them in the next section or in the next book.

Writing sentences

'I can' targets	Section 1	Section 2	Section 3
I can extend sentences to explain, add details or show point of view.	○	○	○
I can use a variety of connectives in sentences (e.g., **if**, **although**, **who**, **which**).	○	○	○
I can reorder and vary sentences (e.g., using adverbs or connectives).		○	○
I can write different types of sentence (e.g., short, long, exclamation, order).			○

Using punctuation

	Section 1	Section 2	Section 3
I can mark the start and end of sentences (using capitals, full stops, ? or!).	○	○	○
I can use commas in lists and to separate adverbs, phrases or sentence parts.	○	○	○
I can use speech marks in dialogue and quotes.	○	○	○
I can use capital letters for a range of purposes.	○	○	○
I can use the apostrophe for possession.		○	○
I can use some more complex punctuation (e.g., dash, hyphen).			○

Checking grammar

	Section 1	Section 2	Section 3
I can write in the past, present or future tense and use **was/were**, **is/are** correctly.	○	○	○
I can keep to the first or the third person in my writing.	○	○	○

Understanding and choosing words

	Section 1	Section 2	Section 3
I can choose precise nouns and adjectives to add detail to my writing.	○	○	○
I can choose adverbs to add interest or impact, or show a point of view.	○	○	○
I can use powerful verbs to show character, create mood and add impact.	○	○	○
I can choose language to match the type of text I am using.	○	○	○
I can use context and knowledge of word parts to work out word meanings.	○	○	○
I can explain the meaning of common homophones.	○	○	○
I can create new words by adding prefixes and suffixes.	○	○	○
I can write interesting similes.		○	○
I can choose interesting words to create atmosphere or humour.		○	○

Spelling

	Section 1	Section 2	Section 3
I can spell words by breaking them into phonemes and syllables.	○	○	○
I can use spelling strategies (e.g., using known words or common patterns).	○	○	○
I can use the apostrophe in shortened forms.	○	○	○
I can spell tricky words (e.g., **walk**).	○	○	○
I can use a dictionary to check the spelling or meaning of a word.	○	○	○
I can choose the correct spelling of homophones (e.g., **hear** and **here**).	○	○	○
I can use the rules for adding verb endings (e.g., **emptied**).	○	○	○
I can use the rules for spelling plurals (e.g., **thieves**).	○	○	○
I can spell words with prefixes (e.g. **al**, **ad**) and suffixes (e.g. **y**, **ive**, **able**).	○	○	○

This page is from **English Skills 3**.

practised in the section. Please ask every pupil to complete the relevant column when they have finished working through a section.

The **Progress chart** encourages pupils to monitor their own work by identifying those activities that they have mastered and those requiring further attention. When pupils colour in the chart as recommended (**green** for **easy**, **orange** for **getting there** and **red** for **difficult**) it gives a clear picture of progress. It also shows the benefits of systematic practice: an activity that the pupil cannot perform in Section 1 later gets the 'green light'.

The **Progress chart** also promotes target setting and further promotes AFL and personalised learning (see page 8). Whilst the **Progress chart** is best completed in the workbook, so that achievements in all sections may be compared, you may at some point wish to have additional copies. For this reason, it may be photocopied. **However, all other pages of the pupil workbook remain strictly non-photocopiable.**

Setting targets

Setting targets helps to ensure that all the knowledge and skills practised in the workbooks is transferred to pupils' own independent reading and writing.

You may wish to use some of the statements from the **Progress chart** as the basis for independent writing targets. Templates for target setting are supplied in this book as photocopy masters (see **General resources: Targets for writing 1**, **2** and **3**). These targets can be made accessible to pupils. For example, they might be displayed on the wall, kept on desks or in writing trays or stuck inside exercise books to remind individuals or groups of the specific improvements that they are aiming for in their own writing.

English Skills helps to create a positive learning environment, developing pupils' confidence and self-esteem and preparing them for full literacy throughout Key Stage 2 and beyond. This is particularly the case when **English Skills** is adopted for whole-school use. Schofield & Sims hopes that you will soon reap the benefits.

Assessment resources

Use these resources to help you decide which **English Skills** workbook a pupil or class should begin with.

Contents

Contents

Glossary

Contents

Schofield & Sims English Skills 3

Glossary

Contents
Schofield & Sims English Skills 4

Glossary

Contents

Glossary

Contents

Glossary

SECTION 1

Tests 1 to 12, covering:

Spelling: Spelling familiar words. Distinguishing homophones. Vowel choices. Tricky letter strings/ phonemes/graphemes. Silent letters. Soft **c** and **g**. Spelling polysyllabic words. Unstressed vowels. Choosing/adding prefixes and suffixes. Pluralisation. **i** before **e**.

Word structure: Identifying roots and affixes; antonym prefixes; meaning of prefixes. Word families. Using suffixes to change word class; choosing the correct suffix.

Vocabulary: Word meanings in different contexts. Archaic language. Word origins. Commonly-confused words.

Sentence structure: Varying sentence length and type; forming complex sentences. Embedding information. Varying sentence construction. Conditional sentences. Using passives.

Punctuation: Using punctuation to mark boundaries between/within sentences. Using apostrophes. Using colons, dashes and semi-colons.

Grammar: Pre- and post-noun modification. Writing inferentially. Using verbs, nouns, adjectives to create effects.

Section 1 Writing task: After hours club

Section 1 Proofreading task: My favourite place

SECTION 2

Tests 1 to 12, covering all the above, plus:

Spelling: Reinforcing spelling rules, complex patterns and exceptions. Choosing endings. Single/ double consonants. Common confusions.

Word structure: Hyphenation. Complex affix formations. Working out meaning using word structure/analogy to known words. Effects of suffixes.

Vocabulary: Using a dictionary/thesaurus. Inferring meaning of unknown words.

Sentence structure: Subordinate clauses using conjunctions, relative pronouns, non-finite verbs. Using modals. Passives to alter focus.

Punctuation: Using sophisticated punctuation in complex sentences/to link ideas. Integrating correctly punctuated speech in longer sentences.

Grammar: Grammatical features of text types. Pronouns. Ambiguity. Adverbs. Standard English. Similes and personification.

Section 2 Writing task: The nervous cyclist

Section 2 Proofreading task: Why we must go green

SECTION 3

Tests 1 to 12, covering all the above, plus:

Spelling: Complex irregular words. Identifying tricky parts. Less-common plural endings. Using analogies to known words/roots. Subject-specific homophones. Commonly-confused words. Identifying misspellings.

Word structure: Lexical patterns relating to suffixes. Using word roots/families to find meanings. Spelling errors related to prefixes/suffixes.

Vocabulary: Using words with precision in different contexts; word class/usage (e.g., words that can be both verbs and nouns; terms of qualification).

Sentence structure: Sentences for specific effects. Avoiding ambiguity.

Punctuation: Punctuation to clarify meaning or create effects.

Grammar: Grammatical confusions (e.g., less/fewer). Visual/sound effects of language. Emotive language. Connectives/text signposts.

Section 3 Writing task: Launchpad local

Section 3 Proofreading task: Megan's mystery

Progress chart

Workbook descriptors for English Skills 1
(equivalent to Year 2)

Word work descriptor

English Skills 1 is for pupils who can recognise most graphemes and know the different ways of spelling phonemes. They can blend phonemes to read words and segment them to spell words. They do not always make the right spelling choice in words.

To progress, these pupils now need to practise:

- building up their knowledge of which words use which spelling alternative
- spelling the less common alternative graphemes used in some words
- spelling irregular or tricky high-frequency (grammatical function) words
- spelling the following endings: regular past tense verbs with **ed**; verbs with **ing**; **s** for regular plurals
- recognising and using some common prefixes and suffixes (for example, **un**, **dis**, **ly**, **ful**)
- spelling two- or three-syllable words, compound words and some simple words with the above prefixes or suffixes.

Sentence work descriptor

English Skills 1 is for pupils who can already write short simple sentences and questions and can use a capital letter and full stop to punctuate single sentences. They mainly use simple, speech-like vocabulary, choosing some words related to the subject.

To progress, these pupils now need to practise:

- extending simple sentences (by using prepositions, for example)
- beginning to form compound sentences using conjunctions (for example, **and**, **but**)
- rereading sentences to check for errors (for example, checking sense and grammatical agreement and ensuring that verb tenses (present and past) are maintained)
- identifying sentence boundaries when writing a sequence of sentences
- punctuating sentences with capital letters at the start and full stops or question marks at the end
- thinking of alternatives for everyday words, sometimes using a more adventurous word to improve a sentence.

Workbook descriptors for English Skills 2 (equivalent to Year 3)

Word work descriptor

English Skills 2 is for pupils who can spell correctly most high-frequency words. They can make plausible attempts at spelling unfamiliar words using their phonic knowledge and other spelling strategies – for example, knowing familiar patterns or saying syllables. They are beginning to build some words using common prefixes and suffixes (for example, **un**, **ful**). They can spell **ing** and **ed** verb endings, although they do not yet fully understand the rules relating to these endings.

To progress, these pupils now need to practise:

- applying the rules for adding **ed** and **ing** (for example, when to double the final consonant, drop the final **e**, change **y** to **i**)

- forming plurals whose spellings change (for example, **es**, **y/ies**)

- recognising a greater range of prefixes (for example, **mis**, **non**) and suffixes (for example, **ly**, **ful**, **less**, **ness**)

- recognising how prefixes change the meaning of words – and using this knowledge to spell words

- changing spelling, where necessary, when adding a suffix such as **y**

- spelling more medium-frequency words

- using apostrophes for omission.

Sentence work descriptor

English Skills 2 is for pupils who can write grammatically accurate simple sentences and use simple conjunctions (for example, **and**, **but**) to write compound sentences. They can demarcate some sentences using capital letters, full stops and question marks and can use capital letters for proper names.

To progress, these pupils now need to practise:

- developing their use of subordinators in relation to time, reason and cause (for example, **while**, **when**, **because**)

- varying the ways in which they open sentences rather than always starting with the subject verb (for example, they might use **where** or **when** starters)

- using precise nouns and adjectives to add detail to their writing and choosing some interesting verbs for impact

- demarcating sentences using capital letters, full stops, **?** and **!**, and securing the use of commas in a list of items, adjectives or phrases

- using inverted commas to distinguish words spoken.

Workbook descriptors for English Skills 3 (equivalent to Year 4)

Word work descriptor

English Skills 3 is for pupils who can correctly spell most words they use regularly and can use strategies and rules to make good attempts at less familiar words (for example, they know the basic rules for adding **ed**, **ing** and **s**). They recognise a range of prefixes and suffixes and can use this knowledge to help them spell words. They know that adding suffixes can sometimes change the spelling as well as the meaning.

To progress, these pupils now need to practise:

- applying the rules for adding suffixes (for example, when forming comparatives or adverbs they need to know when to change **y** to **i**)

- distinguishing the spelling (and meaning) of common homophones (for example, **here**, **hear**)

- spelling tricky medium-frequency words

- using their knowledge of word origins, word roots, prefixes and suffixes, to spell unfamiliar words

- making the link between meaning and spelling.

Sentence work descriptor

English Skills 3 is for pupils who can write simple and compound sentences and use some subordinating conjunctions such as **when** or **because**. They understand what verbs, nouns and adjectives are and are beginning to make some precise and interesting vocabulary choices. They can punctuate sentences with capital letters, full stops, **?** and **!**, and use commas in lists. They are beginning to use speech marks in dialogue and apostrophes in shortened forms. However, they need to be reminded to use punctuation when focusing on composition.

To progress, these pupils now need to practise:

- using a wider range of subordinating conjunctions in their sentences to help link ideas and clarify meaning (for example, **although**, **before**) and using relative clauses

- using phrases and adverbs in their sentences to clarify where, when and how

- moving phrases or adverbials to vary sentence structure (for example, using **how** starters)

- making imaginative language choices to create particular effects – for example, selecting adjectives carefully, creating similes and using powerful verbs to create mood or show character

- punctuating sentences consistently and beginning to use commas to separate phrases, adverbials and clauses in longer sentences

- using apostrophes for possession as well as in shortened forms.

Workbook descriptors for English Skills 4 (equivalent to Year 5)

Word work descriptor

English Skills 4 is for pupils who can spell correctly high- and medium-frequency words and have a range of strategies for spelling unfamiliar words. They know basic spelling rules for adding common inflected endings. They can recognise and spell a good range of prefixes and suffixes and understand how identifying root words can help them to spell a word as well as to understand its meaning.

To progress, these pupils now need to practise:

- learning to spell commonly-used words with unstressed vowels (for example, **interest**)

- recognising less common prefixes and suffixes so they can make appropriate spelling choices (for example, **im**, **ir**; **tion/sion/cian**; **ible/able**)

- consolidating rules for adding vowel and consonant suffixes (for example, drop **e** to add vowel suffix, change **y** to **i** when adding **able**)

- widening their knowledge of word roots to help them spell unfamiliar words as well as understand their meanings.

Sentence work descriptor

English Skills 4 is for pupils who can form simple, compound and some complex sentences. They can use a range of subordinating conjunctions to develop ideas and can add phrases and adverbials to enhance meaning in their sentences. They can vary sentence openings (using **when**, **where** or **how** starters, for example). They can punctuate their writing with full stops, capital letters, question marks, exclamation marks and some commas, although not always consistently – and they may sometimes use a comma where a full stop is needed.

To progress, these pupils now need to practise:

- developing their use of complex sentences by, for example, experimenting with different constructions or different subordinators and learning to use non-finite subordinate clauses

- rearranging parts of sentences for variety or clarity (for example, moving adverbials or subordinate clauses)

- adapting sentence construction and language to different text types, purposes and audiences

- using well-chosen language, including figurative language, for its effect on the reader

- improving their use of commas to separate phrases and clauses within sentences, thereby making meaning clear

- setting out and punctuating direct speech correctly

- correcting errors in the use of apostrophes for possession and contraction

- starting to use some other types of punctuation within sentences (brackets, colon, dash).

Workbook descriptors for English Skills 5 (equivalent to Year 6)

Word work descriptor

English Skills 5 is for pupils whose spelling is mainly accurate – including their spelling of familiar words with unstressed vowels (for example, **interest**, **general**). They can spell words containing prefixes and suffixes, applying the rules for adding vowel and consonant suffixes. They understand the link between meaning and spelling and use their knowledge of word roots and word origins to help them spell many topic words.

To progress, these pupils now need to practise:

- securing their knowledge of spelling rules and learning exceptions to these rules

- correctly spelling subject-specific words with unstressed vowels and consonants and learning spelling patterns relating to unstressed vowels

- further extending their knowledge of word roots, prefixes and suffixes so they can build words from other known words or using their knowledge of the derivation of a word

- building up their word-specific knowledge.

Sentence work descriptor

English Skills 5 is for pupils who can write simple, compound and complex sentences using subordinate clauses (which extend, add information or explain, for example). They can reorder phrases and clauses to add variety or improve clarity (for example, by starting with a subordinating clause). They are beginning to vary sentences and language choices to suit different purposes, audiences and text types. They punctuate sentences fairly consistently and use commas to separate clauses or parts of a sentence.

To progress, these pupils now need to practise:

- manipulating clauses in complex sentences to achieve particular effects (for example, to create surprise)

- forming sentences to express subtle distinctions of meaning (for example, using modal verbs, qualifying words or phrases)

- forming conditional sentences (to express hypothesis, speculation and supposition) and using the passive voice

- using different types of sentence to contribute to the effectiveness of their writing (for example, to vary pace or build suspense)

- using punctuation to clarify meaning within complex sentences – beginning to use semi-colons as well as commas

- using punctuation for effect (for example, dash to create surprise).

Workbook descriptor for English Skills 6
(equivalent to Years 6/7)

English Skills 6 is an extension book for pupils who already have the skills and knowledge outlined in the **English Skills 5** descriptors. This book reinforces the learning acquired in **English Skills 5** and then allows pupils to build on their skills and knowledge.

Word work

To progress, these pupils now need to practise:

- spelling subject-specific words (for example, subject-specific homophones and irregular words)

- avoiding common errors relating to unstressed vowels, hyphenation, similar endings and consonant doubling in more complex words (for example, **occasionally**).

- drawing on analogies to roots, derivations, word families and morphology in order to spell and understand the new words they meet or need

- modifying words to use them in different situations (for example, adding **ify** to an adjective to create a verb).

Sentence work

To progress, these pupils now need to practise:

- making sentence choices that enhance meaning and give clarity to their writing (for example, avoiding ambiguity or changing the focus)

- varying sentence structures to match their purpose and achieve different effects (for example, to appeal, to convey mood, to vary pace or to add emphasis)

- using a range of punctuation to convey and clarify meaning in sentences and texts

- exploring subtle differences between using different forms of punctuation to create particular effects

- matching language choice to their intentions (for example, choosing words for their exact implication in context or experimenting with the visual and/or sound effects of language)

- developing their use of stylistic techniques and devices in different texts.

Schofield & Sims English Skills

Writing sample assessment sheet

Use evidence from any sample of a pupil's writing to help you identify his or her strengths and weaknesses as you complete this assessment sheet.

Name:	Class/Set:
Title of writing sample:	Date:

	Strengths	Next steps
Sentence construction (for example, use simple, compound, complex sentences; vary sentence starters)	Pupil can:	Pupil now needs to:
Punctuation (for example, demarcate sentences; use commas; use speech marks)	Pupil can:	Pupil now needs to:
Grammar and language effects (for example, choose suitable words; use language accurately)	Pupil can:	Pupil now needs to:
Spelling (for example, use strategies, rules, patterns)	Pupil can:	Pupil now needs to:

Name:	Class/Set:

Writing task: Advert for a new car

Task

Write an advertisement for a new car.

Hints

Before you start:

- Think about how you will persuade readers to buy the car.
- What will you tell them about it?
- How will you grab the readers' attention?
- What persuasive tricks could you use?

As you write:

- Consider how writers make adverts persuasive.
- Choose your words carefully.
- Try out phrases and sentences to see if they sound like those in a real advert.

Check

- When you have finished, check through your advert.
- Edit and proofread it.
- Make sure that everything looks and sounds right.

Schofield & Sims English Skills

Writing task assessment sheet: Advert for a new car

Name:	Class/Set:
Teacher's name:	Date:

Sentence structure and punctuation

	Always/ often	Sometimes	Never
Uses simple, compound and complex sentences			
Uses adverbs/phrases/clauses to emphasise/persuade/explain			
Uses various types of sentence (e.g., exclamation, question, order, short sentence for impact)			
Varies sentence openings			
Uses person/tense correctly (e.g., **it has**; **you had**)			
Demarcates sentences accurately			
Uses commas to mark phrases and clauses			
Uses possessive apostrophe correctly			
Uses other punctuation (e.g., dashes)			

Composition and effect

Has a clear sense of purpose to engage with/appeal to the reader			
Different sections are indicated by layout			
Ideas developed logically (e.g., main idea, then detail)			
Makes connections between ideas			
Chooses language for effect (e.g., humour, persuasion)			
Uses expanded noun phrases, adjectives, superlatives			
Chooses powerful verbs for impact			
Uses appropriate tone (e.g., friendly)			

Spelling

Phonically regular words spelt correctly			
Common letter strings are correct			
Tricky high-/medium-frequency words spelt correctly			
Applies rules for adding prefixes/suffixes			
Applies rules for adding verb endings and spelling plurals			
Words with unstressed vowels correct			
Apostrophe used in contracted forms			
Common homophones used correctly			
Other spelling rules applied correctly			

From: **English Skills Teacher's Guide** by Carol Matchett (ISBN 978 0 7217 1187 4). Copyright © Schofield & Sims Ltd, 2011. Published by Schofield & Sims Ltd, Dogley Mill, Fenay Bridge, Huddersfield HD8 0NQ, UK (www.schofieldandsims.co.uk). **This page may be photocopied or printed for use within your school or institution only.**

Name:	Class/Set:

Writing task: Jam sandwich!

Task

A lorry carrying jam crashes in the town centre. Write a newspaper article or report based on this incident. The headline is **Jam sandwich!**

Hints

Before you start:

- Think what the article might be about.
- Consider what your reader will want to know.
- Work out what happened, where, when and why, and who was involved.
- Consider whether there are other vital details that should be included.
- Decide how to organise and set out your article.

As you write:

- Think how a reporter would write the article.
- Choose your words carefully.
- Try out sentences to see if they sound like those in a real newspaper report.

Continue on a separate sheet.

Check

- When you have finished, check through your article.
- Edit and proofread it.
- Make sure that everything looks and sounds right.

From: **English Skills Teacher's Guide** by Carol Matchett (ISBN 978 07217 1187 4). Copyright © Schofield & Sims Ltd, 2011. Published by Schofield & Sims Ltd, Dogley Mill, Fenay Bridge, Huddersfield HD8 0NQ, UK (www.schofieldandsims.co.uk). **This page may be photocopied or printed for use within your school or institution only.**

Writing task assessment sheet: Jam sandwich!

Name:	Class/Set:
Teacher's name:	Date:

Sentence structure and punctuation

	Always/ often	Sometimes	Never
Develops ideas through simple, compound and complex sentences			
Uses varied connectives (e.g., **while**, **after**, **although**)			
Varies sentence construction			
Uses Standard English in news report			
Uses direct and reported speech, punctuated correctly			
Chooses appropriate tense (mainly past)			
Demarcates sentences accurately			
Uses commas to mark grammatical boundaries			
Uses apostrophes correctly			
Shows understanding of other punctuation (e.g., dash)			

Composition and effect

Shows clear sense of purpose			
Uses clearly identifiable sections and paragraphs			
Selects ideas to inform and engage (e.g., vital facts, interesting background information, comments)			
Connectives signal shifts in time, place, focus			
Language chosen for effect (e.g., headlines)			
Uses nouns precisely (e.g., proper nouns, expanded noun phrases)			
Uses powerful verbs for impact and precision			
Uses formal tone and language for newspaper report			

Spelling

Phonically regular words correctly spelt			
Common letter strings correctly spelt (e.g., **ough**)			
Tricky medium-frequency words correct			
Uses rules for adding prefixes and suffixes			
Spells suffixes and word roots correctly			
Applies rules for adding verb endings and spelling plurals			
Words with unstressed vowels correct			
Chooses correct homophone to fit context			
Other spelling rules applied correctly			

English Skills
Entry test 1

Name:

Class: Date:

WORD WORK

1 Complete the list of rhyming words.

    roar   d____   y____   f____   m____

2 Add the missing letters.

    Clue: *found in a non-fiction book*

    i n d _ _   c o n t _ _ _ _ _

Cross out the words that are wrongly spelt.
Write the correct spelling.

3 She startid to showt.

    _____ _____

4 Last nite it snowd.

    _____ _____

5 Thay are haveing a party.

    _____ _____

6 She pickt sum beans.

    _____ _____

Make these words into opposites.

7 lucky and _____

8 agree and _____

9 Make the words in **bold** into plurals.

    Wash all the **plate**____ and **dish**____.

10 Write two compound words that start
with **sun**.

    sun_____   sun_____

SENTENCE WORK

11 Write a sentence using the words **car** and **tree**.

_____

12 Write a question to go with the answer.

_____   Answer: It was sunny every day.

13 Underline the words that are wrong. Write the correct words.

We was going to town but the bus were late.

                                   _____ _____

14 Make the sentence into two separate sentences.

He opened the door and went inside and it was dark.

Finish the sentence in two different ways.

15 The old man was tired so _____

16 The old man was tired but _____

Add the punctuation and capital letters.

17 the fox jumped out the children screamed and ran away

18 who is that at the door it must be jack

19 A word is missing. Give two ideas for what it might be.

Snowflakes _____ to the ground.

                                   _____ _____

Add three more items to the list in the sentence.

20 In my pocket I have a bus ticket, _____

| TOTAL × 5 = PERCENTAGE SCORE | | GIVE PUPIL ENGLISH SKILLS | | ADMINISTER ENTRY TEST | | TOTAL SCORE | |

English Skills
Entry test 2

Name:	
Class:	Date:

WORD WORK

(1) Cross out the verbs in the present tense. Write them in the past tense.

The Prince stops and grabs his sword.

_____ _____

(2) Write each noun as a plural.

puppy   fox   mouse

_____ _____ _____

(3) Add a prefix to make an opposite.

_____tidy   _____honest

_____visible   _____bug

_____-clockwise   _____sense

Cross out the words that are wrongly spelt. Write the correct spelling.

(4) Two lorrys were driveing arownd.

_____ _____ _____

(5) The childrun cryd at such kindnuss.

_____ _____ _____

(6) Its the hotist day ov the yeer!

_____ _____ _____ _____

Add the suffix **y** to make the word an adjective.

(7) crunch _____   luck _____

(8) sun _____   stone _____

Write the shortened form correctly.

(9) dont _____   **(10)** Ive _____

SENTENCE WORK

Cross out the verb and write a better verb to use instead.

(11) Water came out of the pipe. _____

(12) He went through the brambles. _____

Add a word to join the sentences. Do **not** use **and**.

(13) We have lived here _____ I was five.

(14) Jack climbed _____ he reached the top.

(15) Write the notes as one complete sentence.

frog – smooth, moist   toad – dry, rough

_____

(16) Cross out the nouns. Write different nouns to make the sentence more interesting.

A man rode a bike along the road. _____ _____ _____

(17) Write the sentence again using at least three adjectives.

He wore a hat and a cloak made of feathers.

_____

(18) Finish the sentence by adding information that explains.

Don't stand behind a moving swing _____

Add the punctuation and capital letters.

(19) who wants an ice-cream asked melanie

(20) me screamed bobbie and robbie

TOTAL × 5 = PERCENTAGE SCORE	GIVE PUPIL ENGLISH SKILLS	ADMINISTER ENTRY TEST	TOTAL SCORE

English Skills

Entry test 3

Name:

Class: Date:

WORD WORK

1 Underline each root word.

medicine disorderly foolishness

2 Cross out the words that are wrongly spelt.
Write the correct spelling.

Two peeple drouned yesturday in ruff seas.

_____

Complete the table of adjectives.

	comparative	superlative
3 flat		
4 cheeky		

5 Write two words that come from the root
word **horror**.

_____ _____

6 Add a suffix to make the word into
an adjective.

music_____   nut_____

athlete_____   amaze_____   beauty_____

7 Add the suffix **ness** to change the adjective
into a noun.

lovely _____   tidy _____

8 Write the homophone.

stair _____   peace _____

Cross out the word that is wrong.
Write the correct word.

9 Frosty Flakes – a new serial. _____

10 Which colour – red or blew? _____

SENTENCE WORK

11 Rewrite the two sentences as one sentence. Use an adverb in place of the second sentence.

No-one saw him. He was lucky. _____

12 Cross out the verbs and adverb. Write new words to make the character sound different.

Mr Hawkins bounced eagerly into the room and smiled at the class.

_____ _____ _____

13 Extend the sentence using one of these words to start.   **who where that**

They went to the gates _____

14 Continue the sentence to make the point clear.

The litter problem will continue unless _____

15 Extend the sentence so that it says **where**, **why** and **how**.

The man sat _____

16 Reorder the words to make another sentence.

The sun rose slowly over the village. _____

Rewrite the phrase using three words only.

17 the cloak belonging to the actor _____

18 the spaceship belonging to the aliens _____

19 Add the missing punctuation and capital letters.

although it was dark we werent scared well only a bit

20 Add two adjectives to make the planet sound unwelcoming.
Then complete the simile, continuing the same mood.

The surface of the planet was _____ and _____ . The wind felt like _____ .

TOTAL × 5 =
PERCENTAGE SCORE

GIVE PUPIL
ENGLISH SKILLS

ADMINISTER
ENTRY TEST

TOTAL SCORE

From: **English Skills Teacher's Guide** by Carol Matchett (ISBN 978 07217 1187 4). Copyright © Schofield & Sims Ltd, 2011. Published by Schofield & Sims Ltd, Dogley Mill, Fenay Bridge, Huddersfield HD8 0NQ, UK (www.schofieldandsims.co.uk). **This page may be photocopied or printed for use within your school or institution only.**

English Skills

Entry test 4

Name:	
Class:	Date:

WORD WORK

Add a prefix to make the opposite.

(1) ___ human   ___ legal

(2) ___ responsible   ___ probable

(3) Add the correct 'shun' ending.

reduce_____   collide_____

opti _____   electri _____

Add **ible** or **able**.

(4) suit_____   enjoy_____   fashion_____

(5) vis_____   ed_____   horr_____

(6) Write the word correctly.

intrest _____   diffrent _____

(7) Add different suffixes to make four new words.

tune _____

use _____

Cross out the words that are wrongly spelt.
Write the correct spelling.

(8) A terrable beast garded the enterance.

_____

(9) He gave sevral desprate, deafning roars.

_____

(10) Write three words with the root **trans**.

_____

SENTENCE WORK

(11) Add a phrase or clause that gives extra information.

And so, _____, the land of Safara was free once more.

(12) Combine the three sentences into one.

Ursula sold all her hats. She kept one hat. This one hat was Ursula's favourite.

_____

(13) Rewrite the sentence so that the words and/or phrases are in a different order.

Amy forgot her worries for a while huddled by the fire.

_____

(14) Rewrite the sentence as a rhetorical question.

We can all help to save the planet, starting right now.

_____

(15) Complete the sentence in the style of a horror story.

He saw its _____ eyes, round like _____, and its _____ coat of _____ fur.

(16) Write this informal sentence so that it sounds formal.

People shouldn't do things like that. _____

Add punctuation and capital letters so that the text makes sense.

(17) Holding on to the side he kicked his legs the boat moved

(18) Dont drink that screamed josie its jakes magic potion

Continue the sentence after the punctuation mark.

(19) Many objects are made from wood: _____

(20) The door slammed – _____

TOTAL × 5 = PERCENTAGE SCORE		GIVE PUPIL ENGLISH SKILLS		ADMINISTER ENTRY TEST		**TOTAL SCORE**	

From: **English Skills Teacher's Guide** by Carol Matchett (ISBN 978 07217 1187 4). Copyright © Schofield & Sims Ltd, 2011. Published by Schofield & Sims Ltd, Dogley Mill, Fenay Bridge, Huddersfield HD8 0NQ, UK (www.schofieldandsims.co.uk). **This page may be photocopied or printed for use within your school or institution only.**

English Skills

Entry test 5

Name:

Class: Date:

WORD WORK

(1) Add **ei** or **ie**.

p___ce   w___rd   rec___ve

(2) Add **able** or **ible**.

aud_____   detest_____   resist_____

(3) Underline the word that is not correct.
Write it correctly.

purely surely finely truely   _____

(4) Add the missing syllable.

gov___ment lem___ade skel___ton

(5) Write three words using the root word
graph.

_____

(6) Use the **ous** suffix to form adjectives.

grace_____   envy_____   humour_____

Write the correct spelling.

(7) lettice marjerine rasberrys

_____

(8) dictionery factary lottory

_____

(9) tecknolojy airospase intacom

_____

(10) Add an ending to the root to make a word.

bi_____   bio_____   cent_____

uni_____   mono_____   multi_____

SENTENCE WORK

(11) Rearrange the sentence so that the subject comes at the end.

The giant beast slowly loomed out of a thin swirling mist.

_____

(12) Reorder the sentence so that it focuses on the feelings of the character.

He walked on although he was scared. _____

(13) Continue the sentence to form a long complex sentence that builds up suspense.

I followed the path _____

_____

Write two short contrasting sentences to follow the long one that you have just written.

(14) _____

(15) Rewrite the sentence so that it sounds less definite. **In the future we will all have electric cars.**

_____

(16) Rewrite the sentence in the passive form to make it sound impersonal.

I have taken steps to prevent this. _____

(17) Make the sentence into a conditional sentence.

He will be safe _____

Punctuate the sentence so that it sounds effective and the meaning is clear.

(18) They had no key and yet as if by magic slowly so very slowly the door opened.

(19) There carved into the wood was a number 1004.

(20) Punctuate the information as **one** sentence.

On average a person in the UK uses 150 litres of water a day in parts of Africa

each person has just ten litres a day.

TOTAL × 5 =
PERCENTAGE SCORE

GIVE PUPIL
ENGLISH SKILLS

ADMINISTER
ENTRY TEST

TOTAL SCORE

From: **English Skills Teacher's Guide** by Carol Matchett (ISBN 978 07217 1187 4). Copyright © Schofield & Sims Ltd, 2011. Published by Schofield & Sims Ltd, Dogley Mill, Fenay Bridge, Huddersfield HD8 0NQ, UK (www.schofieldandsims.co.uk). **This page may be photocopied or printed for use within your school or institution only.**

English Skills
Entry test 1
marking key

Score	Next steps
0–3	pupil may not yet be ready to start **English Skills**
4–14	give pupil **English Skills 1**
15–20	administer **Entry test 2**

WORD WORK

1 Complete the list of rhyming words.

roar   d <u>oor</u>   y <u>our</u>   f <u>or</u>   m <u>ore</u>

2 Add the missing letters.

Clue: found in a non-fiction book

i n d e<u>e</u> <u>x</u>   c o n t <u>e</u> <u>n</u> <u>t</u> <u>s</u>

Cross out the words that are wrongly spelt.
Write the correct spelling.

3 She ~~startid~~ to ~~showt~~.

<u>started</u>   <u>shout</u>

4 Last ~~nite~~ it ~~snowd~~.

<u>night</u>   <u>snowed</u>

5 ~~Thay~~ are ~~haveing~~ a party.

<u>They</u>   <u>having</u>

6 She ~~pickt~~ ~~sum~~ beans.

<u>picked</u>   <u>some</u>

Make these words into opposites.

7 lucky and <u>unlucky</u>

8 agree and <u>disagree</u>

9 Make the words in **bold** into plurals.

Wash all the **plate**<u>s</u> and **dish**<u>es</u>.

10 Write two compound words that start with **sun**.

sun <u>shine</u>   sun <u>set</u>

Word Focus
1: choosing the correct vowel phoneme
2: spelling two-syllable topic words
3–6: verb endings **ed** and **ing**; regular and tricky high-frequency words
7–8: using prefixes **un** and **dis** to make opposites and negatives
9: adding **s** or **es** to make plurals
10: compound words

SENTENCE WORK

11 Write a sentence using the words **car** and **tree**.

<u>He parked the car by the tree.</u>

12 Write a question to go with the answer.

<u>What was the weather like?</u>   Answer: It was sunny every day.

13 Underline the words that are wrong. Write the correct words.

We <u>was</u> going to town but the bus <u>were</u> late.   <u>were</u>   <u>was</u>

14 Make the sentence into two separate sentences.

He opened the door and went inside. ~~and~~ I̶t was dark.

Finish the sentence in two different ways.

15 The old man was tired so <u>he sat down to rest.</u>

16 The old man was tired but <u>he carried on working.</u>

Add the punctuation and capital letters.

17 T̲he fox jumped out. T̲he children screamed and ran away.

18 W̲ho is that at the door? I̲t must be J̲ack.

19 A word is missing. Give two ideas for what it might be.

Snowflakes _____ to the ground.   <u>drift</u>   <u>float</u>

Add three more items to the list in the sentence.

20 In my pocket I have a bus ticket, <u>a marble, two paper clips and some sweets.</u>

Sentence Focus
11: forming and punctuating simple sentences
12: forming questions; using question marks; spelling question words
13: checking grammatical agreement
14: identifying sentence boundaries; using correct punctuation
15–16: forming compound sentences using conjunctions
17–18: identifying sentences; sentence and question punctuation
19: alternative word choices
20: commas in a list

X DEFINITIVE ANSWER   **X** SAMPLE ANSWER

English Skills
Entry test 2
marking key

Score	Next steps
0–3	give pupil **English Skills 1** for reinforcement; if pupil scored 15–20 on **Entry test 1**, move quickly to **English Skills 2**
4–14	give pupil **English Skills 2**
15–20	administer **Entry test 3**

WORD WORK

1 Cross out the verbs in the present tense. Write them in the past tense.

The Prince ~~stops~~ and ~~grabs~~ his sword.

stopped   _grabbed_

2 Write each noun as a plural.

puppy   fox   mouse

puppies   _foxes_   _mice_

3 Add a prefix to make an opposite.

_un_ tidy   _dis_ honest

_in_ visible   _de_ bug

anti -clockwise   _non_ sense

Cross out the words that are wrongly spelt. Write the correct spelling.

4 Two ~~lorrys~~ were ~~driveing arownd~~.

lorries   _driving_   _around_

5 The ~~childrun cryd~~ at such ~~kindnuss~~.

children   _cried_   _kindness_

6 ~~Its~~ the ~~hotist~~ day ~~ov~~ the ~~yeer~~!

_It's_   _hottest_   _of_   _year_

Add the suffix **y** to make the word an adjective.

7 crunch _crunchy_   luck _lucky_

8 sun _sunny_   stone _stony_

Write the shortened form correctly.

9 dont _don't_   **10** Ive _I've_

1: past tense; adding **ed** and doubling the final consonant
2: spelling plurals
3: using a range of prefixes; word meanings
4–6: proofreading for spelling errors: adding **s**, **ed**, **ing** suffixes; checking medium-frequency words
7–8: adding the suffix **y**
9–10: using apostrophes in shortened forms

SENTENCE WORK

Cross out the verb and write a better verb to use instead.

11 Water ~~came~~ out of the pipe.   _trickled_

12 He ~~went~~ through the brambles.   _scrambled_

Add a word to join the sentences. Do **not** use **and**.

13 We have lived here _since_ I was five.

14 Jack climbed _until_ he reached the top.

15 Write the notes as one complete sentence.

frog – smooth, moist   toad – dry, rough

A frog's skin is smooth and moist but a toad's feels dry and rough.

16 Cross out the nouns. Write different nouns to make the sentence more interesting.

A ~~man~~ rode a ~~bike~~ along the ~~road~~.   _clown_   _unicycle_   _tightrope_

17 Write the sentence again using at least three adjectives.

He wore a hat and a cloak made of feathers.

He wore a floppy hat and a flowing cloak made of multicoloured feathers.

18 Finish the sentence by adding information that explains.

Don't stand behind a moving swing _because it could knock you over._

Add the punctuation and capital letters.

19 "W~~who~~ wants an ice-cream?" asked M~~melanie~~.

20 "M~~me~~!" screamed B~~bobbie~~ and R~~robbie~~.

Sentence Focus
11–12: choosing verbs for precision and impact
13–14: using connectives and subordinators in sentences (time links)
15: linking information within a sentence; sentence punctuation
16: choosing nouns for precision and interest
17: using adjectives for clarity
18: sentences that explain and give reasons; using connectives
19–20: punctuating dialogue: using speech marks, capital letters, full stops, **?** and **!**

X DEFINITIVE ANSWER   **X** SAMPLE ANSWER

From: **English Skills Teacher's Guide** by Carol Matchett (ISBN 978 07217 1187 4). Copyright © Schofield & Sims Ltd, 2011. Published by Schofield & Sims Ltd, Dogley Mill, Fenay Bridge, Huddersfield HD8 0NQ, UK (www.schofieldandsims.co.uk). **This page may be photocopied or printed for use within your school or institution only.**

Entry test 3 marking key

Score	Next steps
0–3	give pupil **English Skills 2** for reinforcement; if pupil scored 15–20 on **Entry test 2**, move quickly to **English Skills 3**
4–14	give pupil **English Skills 3**
15–20	administer **Entry test 4**

WORD WORK

1 Underline each root word.

medicine dis<u>orderly</u> <u>foolishness</u>

2 Cross out the words that are wrongly spelt. Write the correct spelling.

Two ~~peeple drouned yesturday~~ in ~~ruff~~ seas.

people drowned yesterday rough

Complete the table of adjectives.

	comparative	superlative
3 **flat**	flatter	flattest
4 **cheeky**	cheekier	cheekiest

5 Write two words that come from the root word **horror**.

horrific   horrible

6 Add a suffix to make the word into an adjective.

music al   nut ty

athlete ic   amaze ing   beauty iful

7 Add the suffix **ness** to change the adjective into a noun.

lovely loveliness   tidy tidiness

8 Write the homophone.

stair stare   peace piece

Cross out the word that is wrong. Write the correct word.

9 Frosty Flakes – a new ~~serial.~~ cereal

10 Which colour – red or ~~blew?~~ blue

Word Focus
1: identifying root words, prefixes and suffixes
2: checking spelling of tricky words
3–4: forming comparatives and superlatives; rules for adding suffixes
5: knowledge of word roots
6: knowledge of suffixes and spelling rules for adding them
7: forming words with suffixes; spelling rules
8–10: homophones

SENTENCE WORK

11 Rewrite the two sentences as one sentence. Use an adverb in place of the second sentence.

No-one saw him. He was lucky. Luckily, no-one saw him.

12 Cross out the verbs and adverb. Write new words to make the character sound different.

Mr Hawkins ~~bounced eagerly~~ into the room and ~~smiled~~ at the class.

stormed   angrily   glared

13 Extend the sentence using one of these words to start. **who where that**

They went to the gates where they had been told to wait.

14 Continue the sentence to make the point clear.

The litter problem will continue unless we have more bins.

15 Extend the sentence so that it says **where**, **why** and **how**.

The man sat quietly on the park bench waiting for his wife.

16 Reorder the words to make another sentence.

The sun rose slowly over the village. Slowly, the sun rose over the village.

Rewrite the phrase using three words only.

17 the cloak belonging to the actor the actor's cloak

18 the spaceship belonging to the aliens the aliens' spaceship

19 Add the missing punctuation and capital letters.

A
although it was dark, we weren't scared. W well, only a bit.

20 Add two adjectives to make the planet sound unwelcoming. Then complete the simile, continuing the same mood.

The surface of the planet was icy and bare . The wind felt like freezing knives .

Sentence Focus
11: forming and placing adverbs in sentences; spelling adverbs and changing **y** to **i**
12: choosing language for effect: verbs and adverbs to show character
13: using relative clauses
14: using conjunctions to expand and clarify
15: adding phrases and adverbs to clarify
16: varying sentences: moving adverbs or phrases; use of commas
17–18: possessive apostrophes
19: checking sentence punctuation; use of commas
20: selecting adjectives and forming similes to create mood

X DEFINITIVE ANSWER   **X** SAMPLE ANSWER

English Skills
Entry test 4 marking key

Score	Next steps
0–3	give pupil **English Skills 3** for reinforcement; if pupil scored 15–20 on **Entry test 3**, move quickly to **English Skills 4**
4–14	give pupil **English Skills 4**
15–20	administer **Entry test 5**

WORD WORK

Add a prefix to make the opposite.

1 _in_ human   _il_ legal

2 _ir_ responsible   _im_ probable

3 Add the correct 'shun' ending.

reduce _tion_   collide _sion_

opti _cian_   electri _cian_

Add **ible** or **able**.

4 suit _able_   enjoy _able_   fashion _able_

5 vis _ible_   ed _ible_   horr _ible_

6 Write the word correctly.

intrest _interest_   diffrent _different_

7 Add different suffixes to make four new words.

tune _tuneful tuneless tuning tuned_

use _useful useless user using_

Cross out the words that are wrongly spelt. Write the correct spelling.

8 A ~~terrable~~ beast ~~garded~~ the ~~enterance.~~
terrible guarded entrance

9 He gave ~~sevral desprate, deafning~~ roars.
several desperate deafening

10 Write three words with the root **trans**.
transplant transfer transmit

Word Focus
1–2: using less common prefixes to form opposites (**in, il, ir, im**)
3: using **tion, sion** and **cian**
4–5: spelling choice: **able** and **ible**
6: spelling unstressed vowels
7: rules for adding suffixes
8–9: spelling unstressed vowels
10: knowledge of word roots

SENTENCE WORK

11 Add a phrase or clause that gives extra information.

And so, _thanks to Prince Alfonso_ , the land of Safara was free once more.

12 Combine the three sentences into one.

Ursula sold all her hats. She kept one hat. This one hat was Ursula's favourite.
Ursula sold all her hats except one, which was her favourite.

13 Rewrite the sentence so that the words and/or phrases are in a different order.

Amy forgot her worries for a while huddled by the fire.
Huddled by the fire, Amy forgot her worries for a while.

14 Rewrite the sentence as a rhetorical question.

We can all help to save the planet, starting right now.
Shouldn't we all be doing our bit to save the planet?

15 Complete the sentence in the style of a horror story.

He saw its _fearsome_ eyes, round like _saucers_ , and its _filthy_ coat of _matted_ fur.

16 Write this informal sentence so that it sounds formal.

People shouldn't do things like that. _Such behaviour is totally unacceptable._

Add punctuation and capital letters so that the text makes sense.

17 Holding on to the side, he kicked his legs. The boat moved.

18 "Don't drink that!" screamed Josie. "It's Jake's magic potion!"

Continue the sentence after the punctuation mark.

19 Many objects are made from wood: _tables, shelves, cupboards and pencils._

20 The door slammed – _they were trapped!_

Sentence Focus
11: embedding a phrase or clause using commas
12: forming and punctuating a complex sentence
13: reordering sentences; using commas
14: adapting sentence types
15: choosing language for effect
16: using formal and informal language
17: using commas and full stops; making meaning clear
18: punctuating direct speech; using apostrophes
19–20: using punctuation within sentences: colons, commas and dashes

X DEFINITIVE ANSWER   **X** SAMPLE ANSWER

From: **English Skills Teacher's Guide** by Carol Matchett (ISBN 978 07217 1187 4). Copyright © Schofield & Sims Ltd, 2011. Published by Schofield & Sims Ltd, Dogley Mill, Fenay Bridge, Huddersfield HD8 0NQ, UK (www.schofieldandsims.co.uk). **This page may be photocopied or printed for use within your school or institution only.**

English Skills
Entry test 5 marking key

Score	Next steps
0–3	give pupil **English Skills 4** for reinforcement; if pupil scored 15–20 on **Entry test 4**, move quickly to **English Skills 5**
4–14	give pupil **English Skills 5**
15–20	give pupil **English Skills 5** for reinforcement; move quickly to **English Skills 6**

WORD WORK

1 Add **ei** or **ie**.

p _ie_ ce   w _ei_ rd   rec _ei_ ve

2 Add **able** or **ible**.

aud _ible_   detest _able_   resist _ible_

3 Underline the word that is not correct. Write it correctly.

purely surely finely <u>truely</u>   _truly_

4 Add the missing syllable.

gov _ern_ ment   lem _on_ ade   skel _e_ ton

5 Write three words using the root word **graph**.

graphic photograph telegraph

6 Use the **ous** suffix to form adjectives.

grace _ious_   envy _ious_   humou~~r~~ _ous_

Write the correct spelling.

7 lettice marjerine rasberrys

lettuce margarine raspberries

8 dictionery factary lottory

dictionary factory lottery

9 tecknolojy airospase intacom

technology aerospace intercom

10 Add an ending to the root to make a word.

bi _cycle_   bio _logy_   cent _igrade_

uni _corn_   mono _gram_   multi _media_

Word Focus
1: using the **i** before **e** spelling rule and exceptions to it
2: using the **ible/able** spelling rule and exceptions to it
3: rules for adding suffixes and exceptions
4: words with unstressed vowels or consonants
5: knowledge of word roots and derivations
6: rules for adding suffixes and exceptions
7–8: correcting unstressed vowels and consonants
9: using knowledge of word roots to correct spelling
10: building words from roots

SENTENCE WORK

11 Rearrange the sentence so that the subject comes at the end.

The giant beast slowly loomed out of a thin swirling mist.

Slowly, out of a thin swirling mist, loomed the giant beast.

12 Reorder the sentence so that it focuses on the feelings of the character.

He walked on although he was scared. _Although he was scared, he walked on._

13 Continue the sentence to form a long complex sentence that builds up suspense.

I followed the path _as it twisted through the sinister tangle of branches, leading me into the heart of the forest._

Write two short contrasting sentences to follow the long one that you have just written.

14 _Something moved. What was it?_

15 Rewrite the sentence so that it sounds less definite. **In the future we will all have electric cars.**

Perhaps in the future we might all have electric cars.

16 Rewrite the sentence in the passive form to make it sound impersonal.

I have taken steps to prevent this. _Steps have been taken to prevent this._

17 Make the sentence into a conditional sentence.

He will be safe _as long as no-one sees_ him.

Punctuate the sentence so that it sounds effective and the meaning is clear.

18 They had no key and yet, as if by magic, slowly, so very slowly, the door opened.

19 There, carved into the wood, was a number: 1004.

20 Punctuate the information as **one** sentence.

On average, a person in the UK uses 150 litres of water a day; in parts of Africa, each person has just ten litres a day.

Sentence Focus
11–12: reordering sentences for effect; using commas
13–14: varying types of sentence for effect; juxtaposing long and short sentences
15: modal verbs or qualifying words for precise meaning
16: using passive forms in impersonal writing
17: using conditional sentences
18: using punctuation for effect (e.g. commas, dashes)
19: using punctuation to clarify meaning (e.g. commas, colons)
20: using commas and semi-colons

X DEFINITIVE ANSWER   **X** SAMPLE ANSWER

General resources

Use these resources as your pupils begin working through the **English Skills** workbooks.

Every resource in this section may be photocopied after purchase for use within your school or institution only.

Schofield & Sims English Skills

Group record sheet

Teacher's name:

Class/Set:

Date started:

Date finished:

Pupil/student names:	Highest Entry test taken	Entry test result	Book number	Section 1 Test 1	Section 1 Test 2	Section 1 Test 3	Section 1 Test 4	Section 1 Test 5	Section 1 Test 6	Section 1 Test 7	Section 1 Test 8	Section 1 Test 9	Section 1 Test 10	Section 1 Test 11	Section 1 Test 12	Section 1 Writing	Section 1 Proofreading	Section 2 Test 1	Section 2 Test 2	Section 2 Test 3	Section 2 Test 4	Section 2 Test 5	Section 2 Test 6	Section 2 Test 7	Section 2 Test 8	Section 2 Test 9	Section 2 Test 10	Section 2 Test 11	Section 2 Test 12	Section 2 Writing	Section 2 Proofreading	Section 3 Test 1	Section 3 Test 2	Section 3 Test 3	Section 3 Test 4	Section 3 Test 5	Section 3 Test 6	Section 3 Test 7	Section 3 Test 8	Section 3 Test 9	Section 3 Test 10	Section 3 Test 11	Section 3 Test 12	Section 3 Writing	Section 3 Proofreading

From: *English Skills Teacher's Guide* by Carol Matchett (ISBN 978 07217 1187 4). Copyright © Schofield & Sims Ltd, 2011. Published by Schofield & Sims Ltd, Dogley Mill, Fenay Bridge, Huddersfield HD8 0NQ, UK (www.schofieldandsims.co.uk).
This page may be photocopied or printed for use within your school or institution only.

Schofield & Sims English Skills

Generic spelling sheet 1: Spelling wall

Name:	Class/Set:
Date started:	Date finished:

Fill this wall with the words you want to learn to spell. Tick each word as you learn to spell it.

From: **English Skills Teacher's Guide** by Carol Matchett (ISBN 978 07217 1187 4). Copyright © Schofield & Sims Ltd, 2011. Published by Schofield & Sims Ltd, Dogley Mill, Fenay Bridge, Huddersfield HD8 0NQ, UK (www.schofieldandsims.co.uk). **This page may be photocopied or printed for use within your school or institution only.**

Generic spelling sheet 2:
Personal spelling list

Name:	Class/Set:
Date started:	Date finished:

Make a list of the words you want to learn.

Word	How will you remember it?	Test yourself				

Spelling strategies checklist

Stuck on how to spell a word? Have a go using the tips below.
You can always check the word later.

Strategy 1: Phonemes

Say the word and segment the phonemes (for example, **sh-r-i-n-k**).

Strategy 2: Syllables

Say the syllables and spell each syllable (for example, **re/mem/ber**).

Strategy 3: Analogy

Think of other words that sound the same (for example, **night**, **bright**, **slight**).

Strategy 4: Root words

Identify the root word and the prefixes and suffixes added to it (for example, **un/like/ly**).

Strategy 5: Rules

If there is a spelling rule to help you, use it (for example, **carry ied**).

Still not sure?

Strategy 6: Experiment

Write the word in several different ways and see which looks right.

Strategy 7: Spelling log

Look in your spelling log; refer to charts or lists.

Strategy 8: Dictionary

Use a dictionary.

Schofield & Sims English Skills

Name:

Class/Set:

Spelling rules

Try to remember these spelling rules.

Rule:

Examples:

Rule:

Examples:

Rule:

Examples:

Rule:

Examples:

Rule:

Examples:

Name:	Class/Set:

Learn to spell a word

Use this simple method for learning how to spell a word.

Look	First you look at the word.
Say	Then you say it. Is there a tricky bit? If so, underline the tricky bit to help you remember it.
Cover	Now cover the word.
Write	Try to write the word while it is still covered up. Think carefully about the tricky bit.
Check	Finally, check your spelling to see if you are right.

Now try it. Use the space below to write and rewrite the spellings you want to learn.

Write the spelling you want to learn in the first column. Then cover and write it three times. Put a tick in the 'Learnt it!' column when you can spell the word.

Look and say	Cover and write 1	Cover and write 2	Cover and write 3	Learnt it!

Proofreading checklist 1: Spelling

When you are proofreading your writing, remember to check for spelling errors.
Use this checklist to help you.

Step 1: Look

Look carefully at the words. Do they look right? Underline any words that look wrong.

Step 2: Targets

Think about your spelling targets. Have you remembered them? Put any words right.

Step 3: Underline

Look at the words you think are wrong. Underline the part of the word that looks wrong.
Why does it look wrong?

Step 4: Alternatives

Try an alternative spelling. Does that look right?

Step 5: Spelling log

Look for some help – for example, in your spelling log, on word lists around the room,
in a dictionary – or ask a friend.

Step 6: Write it

Write in the correct spelling.

Step 7: Remember

Try to remember the correct spelling so you can spell it right next time.

From: **English Skills Teacher's Guide** *by Carol Matchett (ISBN 978 07217 1187 4). Copyright © Schofield & Sims Ltd, 2011. Published by Schofield & Sims Ltd, Dogley Mill, Fenay Bridge, Huddersfield HD8 0NQ, UK (www.schofieldandsims.co.uk).* **This page may be photocopied or printed for use within your school or institution only.**

Proofreading checklist 2: Punctuation

Remember to proofread your writing to check the punctuation. Follow these steps.

Step 1: Read and listen for breaks between sentences

Read your writing aloud or aloud in your head. Listen for the end of each sentence.
Have you put a capital letter at the start of each sentence and a full stop, question mark
or exclamation mark at the end?

Step 2: Read and listen for breaks within sentences

Read your longer sentences carefully. Listen for breaks within the sentence.
Have you put commas to separate parts of the sentence (for example, clauses or phrases)?

Step 3: Check dialogue

Check any dialogue you have written. Read and listen for the words that are spoken.
Have you used speech marks round the words spoken?

Step 4: Check apostrophes

Look carefully at where you have used apostrophes. Have you put them in the right places?
Have you forgotten any apostrophes in shortened forms or apostrophes for possession?

Step 5: Check punctuation and meaning

Have a final read through. Follow the clues given by your punctuation. Does the punctuation help
to make your meaning clear?

From: **English Skills Teacher's Guide** by Carol Matchett (ISBN 978 07217 1187 4). Copyright © Schofield & Sims Ltd, 2011. Published by Schofield & Sims Ltd, Dogley Mill, Fenay Bridge, Huddersfield HD8 0NQ, UK (www.schofieldandsims.co.uk). **This page may be photocopied or printed for use within your school or institution only.**

Punctuation prompt 1

Here are some common punctuation marks. Check that you remember their names.

Read the example sentence. This will remind you how the punctuation mark is used.

Full stop . Put a full stop at the end of a sentence.	**Question mark** ? What do you put at the end of a question?
Exclamation mark ! Exclamation marks are so exciting!	**Comma** , Of course, if you write a longer sentence, you might need a comma or two.
Speech marks " " "Remember to use speech marks," said the teacher.	**Apostrophe** ' Don't forget apostrophes. They're really important.

Punctuation prompt 2

Here are some more punctuation marks. Check that you remember their names.

Read the example sentence. This will remind you how the punctuation mark is used.

Colon **:** A colon has many uses: to start a list, before a quote, to lead into an example or to add a piece of information.	**Semi-colon** **;** A semi-colon is stronger than a comma; it is not as strong as a full stop.
Dash **—** A dash can be used to add an extra thought or comment – like this.	**Pair of commas** **, ,** Use a pair of commas, like these, to add extra information in the middle of a sentence.
Hyphen **-** A hyphen links two words. It is word-friendly.	**Brackets** **( )** Brackets are always used in pairs. Use a pair of brackets (like these) to add extra information to the middle of a sentence.

Name: | Class/Set:

Vocabulary collection 1: **Word collector**

Use this sheet to collect interesting new words to use in your writing.
Some examples are given to help you make a start.

vivid verbs

jostled

quiver

hurtle

adorable adjectives

ravenous

perplexed

malicious

adventurous adverbs

curiously

cautiously

wildly

new nouns

torrent

enthusiast

unicycle

Name:

Class/Set:

Vocabulary collection 2: Synonym collector

Use this sheet to collect interesting new words to use in your writing.
Some examples are given to help you make a start.

said	**walked**
whispered	strolled
looked	**took**
stared	grabbed

From: **English Skills Teacher's Guide** by Carol Matchett (ISBN 978 07217 1187 4). Copyright © Schofield & Sims Ltd, 2011. Published by Schofield & Sims Ltd, Dogley Mill, Fenay Bridge, Huddersfield HD8 0NQ, UK (www.schofieldandsims.co.uk). **This page may be photocopied or printed for use within your school or institution only.**

Name: Class/Set:

Vocabulary collection 3: Adjective collector

Use this sheet to collect interesting new words to use in your writing.
Some examples are given to help you make a start.

bright gleaming	**dull** gloomy
small minute	**large** elephantine

From: **English Skills Teacher's Guide** by Carol Matchett (ISBN 978 07217 1187 4). Copyright © Schofield & Sims Ltd, 2011. Published by Schofield & Sims Ltd, Dogley Mill, Fenay Bridge, Huddersfield HD8 0NQ, UK (www.schofieldandsims.co.uk). **This page may be photocopied or printed for use within your school or institution only.**

Sentence prompt

When you write a sentence, remember to:

think it,

say it

and try to improve it.

When you like it ...

... then write it!

Writer's toolbox

As you plan and begin your writing, remember to select the tools that you need for the task.

powerful verbs	for example, **stormed**, **glowered**
nouns to name precisely	for example, a **Dalmatian**, a **cottage**
adjectives to describe	for example, **dazzling**, **fearsome**
'wow' words	for example, **astounding**, **grotesque**
adverbs to say how	for example, **swiftly**, **nervously**
similes	for example, **as round as a balloon**
metaphors	for example, **the sky was a cloak of black velvet**
long sentences	for example, **As the rest of the team joked and chatted, I shivered with the cold, nervously awaiting kick-off.**
short sentences	for example, **He waited.**
sentence starters	**where** starters: for example, **Down by the river**
	when starters: for example, **Meanwhile**
	how starters: for example, **Slowly**
	why starters: for example, **Because it was late**
	ing starters: for example, **Racing along the road**

Schofield & Sims English Skills

Name:	Class/Set:

Targets for writing 1: Target setting

Write down your targets for writing. Put a tick in the next box every time you achieve the target in a piece of writing.

My targets for writing are …

- I must _____

  _____

- I must _____

  _____

- I must _____

  _____

- I must _____

  _____

Name:	Class/Set:

Targets for writing 2: Colour the target

When I am writing I must remember to …

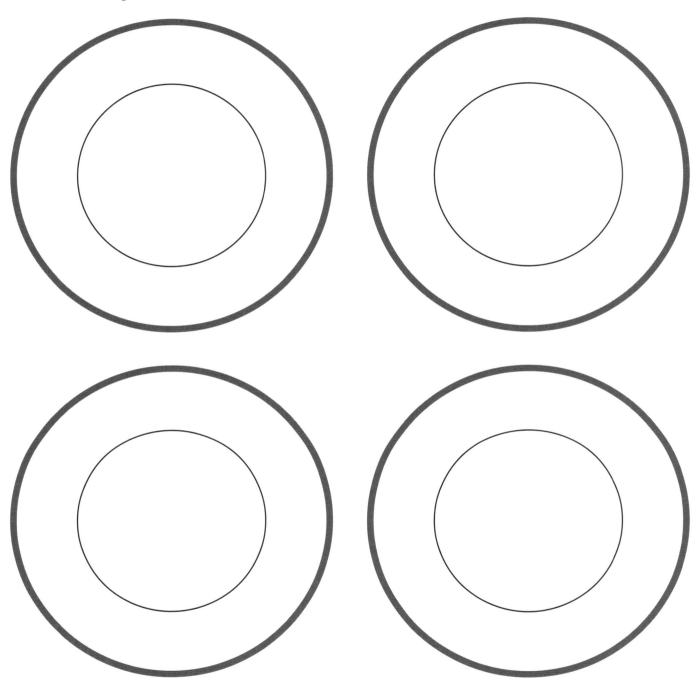

Write your target in the centre of the circle, using a dark pen or crayon.
Colour the outside of the target to show that you are getting there.
Colour the centre when you achieve the target.

Schofield & Sims English Skills

Name:	Class/Set:

Targets for writing 3: Record sheet

Use this sheet to keep a record of your writing targets.

Target	Date set	Date achieved

Glossary

abstract noun — the name of a thought, idea, quality or emotion (e.g., **happiness**)

acronym — a word formed from the first letters of other words (e.g., the acronym **pin** stands for **personal identification number**)

acrostic — a poem, phrase or sentence in which the first letters of each line or word spell out a word of special significance (e.g., the poem's subject)

active — where the subject of the sentence performs the action (e.g., in the active sentence **The dog chased the cat**, the dog is the subject and performs the action) (*compare* **passive**)

adjective — a describing word giving extra information about a noun (e.g., **huge**, **squashy**)

adverb — a word that says more about a verb or sentence, such as **how** or **when** (e.g., **slowly**, **unfortunately**)

adverbial phrase — a group of words that act like an adverb by saying where, when or how (e.g., He arrived **a few days ago**.)

affix — a group of letters added to a word – at the beginning (prefix) or at the end (suffix)

alliteration — a sound pattern in which several words begin with the same letter (e.g., **B**ert **b**lows **b**ig **b**ubbles)

alphabetical order — words put in the same order as the letters of the alphabet (e.g., **ant**, **ball**)

ambiguity — where a sentence or phrase could have more than one possible meaning (e.g., **old boys' school**)

anagram — a word puzzle where the letters of a word have been mixed up

antonym — a word with the opposite meaning (e.g., **soft** and **hard** are antonyms) (*see also* **opposites**; *compare* **synonym**)

apostrophe — looks like this **'** and is used in shortened forms of words (e.g., **can't**) or to show possession (e.g., **the man's hat**)

brackets — look like this **()** and are used to add extra information to a sentence

capital letter — a special way of writing letters (e.g., a capital **a** looks like this: **A**)

caption — a title that tells you what a picture shows

character — a person in a story. Some stories have animal characters.

clause — a part of a sentence. It includes a verb.

cliché — an overused phrase, saying or simile

colon — looks like this **:** and is used to introduce a list, a quote or a second clause

comma — looks like this **,** and is used to separate parts of a sentence

comparative adjective — a describing word that is used to compare two items (e.g., **smaller**, **faster**)

complex sentence — a sentence with a main clause and one or more subordinate clauses

compound sentence — a sentence where two equal clauses are joined with **and**, **but** or **so** (e.g., It was late **and** he was tired.)

compound word — a word made from two smaller words (e.g., **something**)

conditional sentence	a sentence where one thing depends on another (e.g., **If** it rains we **might** get wet.)
conjunction	a word used to join the parts of a sentence (e.g., **when**, **while**, **because**)
connective	a word that links two pieces of information in a sentence (e.g., **when**, **while**, **because**) or a word that links two different sentences (e.g., **meanwhile**)
dash	a long line that looks like this – and is used to add extra information to a sentence
definition	a sentence or phrase that gives the meaning of a word
derivation	where a word comes from (e.g., the derivation of the word **public** is the Latin word **publicum**, meaning 'of the people')
describing word	a word that helps you to say what something is like (*see also* **adjective**)
dictionary	a book of words arranged in alphabetical order. You can use it to check the spelling and the meaning of a word as long as you know the first few letters.
direct speech	a written version of the exact words spoken, which appear in speech marks (e.g., **"I am very tired,"** said Annie.)
e.g.	a short way of writing **for example**
embed	to add extra information to the middle of a sentence (e.g., in the sentence **Daniel James, aged 10, was the winner**, the **aged 10** has been embedded)
exclamation	a sentence with strong feeling (e.g., I won!)
exclamation mark	looks like this **!** and is used at the end of exclamations
fact	something that is definitely true and can be proved
fiction	writing that is made up (*compare* **non-fiction**)
first person	writing about yourself, using **I** or **we**
formal language	the language and sentence structure that we use in special 'formal' situations (*compare* **informal language**)
full stop	looks like this **.** and is used at the end of a sentence
glossary	a list, like this one, which explains the meaning of specialist or technical words. The words are listed in alphabetical order.
grapheme	the letter or letters that represent a sound
haiku	a poem with three lines that is made up of 17 syllables in total (5, 7, 5)
homonym	a word with the same spelling as another word, but a different meaning
homophone	a word that sounds the same as another but has a different meaning and/or spelling (e.g., **two**, **too** and **to** are homophones)
hyphen	a short line that looks like this **-** and is used to join the two parts of some compound words (e.g., **mix-up**)
idiom	an expression that is not meant to be taken literally (e.g., the idiom **a piece of cake** refers to a task that is easy to complete; it has nothing to do with cake)
imagery	the use of language to create vivid images (e.g., **similes**, **metaphors**)
imperative	a command or order (e.g., Give that to me!)
informal language	the everyday language and sentence structure that we use with people we know. When written down, informal language is similar to spoken language. (*compare* **formal language**)

instructions	writing that tells you how to do something
label	words attached to something. The label tells you what it is.
metaphor	a comparison that does **not** use **like** or **as** (e.g., The moon was a silver coin.) (*compare* **simile**)
mnemonic	a literary device that helps you to remember something (e.g., the mnemonic **Rhythm helps your two hips move** helps you to spell the word **rhythm**)
modal verb	a verb form such as **can**, **shall** or **might**, which is used with other verbs to express shades of meaning (e.g., We **might** meet again.)
non-fiction	writing that is based on fact (*compare* **fiction**)
non-finite verb	a verb that does not show the tense (e.g., **falling** to the ground)
notes	key words used as a reminder. Notes are not written as full sentences.
noun	a naming word. Nouns name objects, people and places (e.g., **book**, **nurse**, **library**).
noun phrase	a group of words built around the noun or naming word (e.g., **the new library**)
onomatopoeia	a word that sounds like the noise it describes (e.g., **pop**, **sizzle**)
opinion	a belief that is not definitely true and cannot be proved
opposites	words that mean completely different things (e.g., **hot** and **cold**) (*see also* **antonym**)
passive	where the subject of the sentence receives the action (e.g., in the passive sentence **The cat was chased by the dog**, the cat is the subject and receives the action) (*compare* **active**)
past tense	when something has already happened (e.g., We **went** to school.)
person	the first person is **I** or **we**, the second is **you**, the third is **he**, **she**, **it** or **they**
personification	a metaphor where a non-human subject is described in human terms (e.g., The sun smiled down on the fields.)
phoneme	a sound made by one, two or three letters
phrase	a group of words that go together, a part of a sentence
plural	more than one of something (e.g., **cats**)
prefix	a group of letters added to the start of some words (e.g., **un**, **dis**) (*compare* **suffix**)
preposition	a word that is usually followed by a noun phrase. Many prepositions tell you about time, position or direction (e.g., **at**, **under**, **between**, **over**).
pronoun	a word used in place of a noun (e.g., **he**, **his**, **theirs**)
proper noun	the name of a person, place or organisation (e.g., **Dr Naidoo**, **Wales**, the **BBC**)
proverb	a saying that teaches you something about life (e.g., Better safe than sorry.)
pun	a humorous play on words, often involving the deliberate use of homophones. You use on purpose words that sound the same but have different meanings (e.g., Where do polar bears vote? The North Poll!)
punctuation	marks such as full stops and question marks, which are used in writing
question mark	looks like this **?** and is used at the end of a sentence that asks something
recount	writing that is about an event. It says what happened.

relative clause	a subordinate clause that begins with a relative pronoun, such as **who**, **which**, **whose** or **that** (e.g., **which** I hated) (*see also* **subordinate clause**)
report	writing that gives information about a subject
reported speech	a written version of words spoken, in which you report what was said without using the actual words (e.g., Annie said she was very tired.)
rhetorical question	a question that is used for effect rather than to be answered (e.g., Why me?)
rhyming couplet	two lines that follow each other and end with words that rhyme
rhyming words	words that have the same sound at the end (e.g., **bed**, **said**, **bread**)
root word	a word that can have prefixes and suffixes added to it to make more words (e.g., the root word **play** can be made into **replay** or **playful**)
semi-colon	looks like this **;** and is used to separate parts of a sentence
simile	a descriptive comparison in which a writer compares one thing to another using the words **like** or **as** (e.g., **he swims like a fish** or **as big as an elephant**) (*compare* **metaphor**)
speech marks	look like this **" "**. They go either side of any words that are spoken (e.g., "My name is Jack," he said.)
Standard English	the accepted rules and patterns of written English (e.g., you might say **There was this man** but in Standard English you would write **There was a man**)
story	a made-up series of events
subordinate clause	a clause that would not make sense on its own but provides extra information
suffix	a group of letters added to the end of the word (e.g., **ful**, **ly**) (*compare* **prefix**)
syllable	a small part of a longer word. Each syllable makes a separate sound or beat when you say the word (e.g., **fol / low / ing** has three syllables).
synonym	a word with a similar meaning (e.g., **cold** is a synonym of **chilly**) (*compare* **antonym**)
thesaurus	a book of synonyms, which lists words with similar meanings
third person	writing about someone else (e.g., **he**, **she**, **they**)
transcript	a written copy
verb	a doing word (e.g., **catch**, **throw**, **run**, **jump**) or a being word (e.g., **was** or **is**)
verb tense	a verb (doing word) can be written in the past, present or future tense, e.g., I **played** (past), I **play** (present) and I **will play** (future)
vowel	the special sound made by certain letters. The letters **a**, **e**, **i**, **o** and **u** make short vowel sounds. Long vowel sounds are made by putting letters together (e.g., **ai**, **igh**).
word class	the type of word (e.g., verb, noun, adjective, adverb, pronoun)

Full list of the Schofield & Sims English Skills books

Workbooks

For Key Stage 2:

English Skills 1	978 07217 1175 1
English Skills 2	978 07217 1176 8
English Skills 3	978 07217 1177 5
English Skills 4	978 07217 1178 2
English Skills 5	978 07217 1179 9
English Skills 6	978 07217 1180 5

The same workbooks, with covers designed for older users – at Key Stage 3 and beyond:

Essential English Skills 1	978 07217 1188 1
Essential English Skills 2	978 07217 1189 8
Essential English Skills 3	978 07217 1190 4
Essential English Skills 4	978 07217 1191 1
Essential English Skills 5	978 07217 1192 8
Essential English Skills 6	978 07217 1193 5

Answers

Suitable for use with both **English Skills** and **Essential English Skills**:

English Skills 1 Answers	978 07217 1181 2
English Skills 2 Answers	978 07217 1182 9
English Skills 3 Answers	978 07217 1183 6
English Skills 4 Answers	978 07217 1184 3
English Skills 5 Answers	978 07217 1185 0
English Skills 6 Answers	978 07217 1186 7

Teacher's Guide

This **Teacher's Guide** contains the **Workbook descriptors**, **Entry tests** and many other useful items suitable for use with both **English Skills** and **Essential English Skills**:

English Skills Teacher's Guide	978 07217 1187 4

Also available

Mental Arithmetic (for Key Stage 2) and **Essential Mental Arithmetic** (for Key Stage 3 and beyond) are similar in format to **English Skills** and **Essential English Skills**, providing intensive maths practice.

 For further information about both series, and for details of the **I can do** teaching method, which can be used with all the books mentioned on this page, visit **www.schofieldandsims.co.uk**